# Baby Names

## *inspired by Mother Nature*

*By Veronika Sophia Robinson*

Baby names inspired by Mother Nature
*Written by Veronika Sophia Robinson*

Published by Starflower Press
www.starflowerpress.com
ISBN: 978-0-9560344-8-9
© Veronika Sophia Robinson
© Illustrations by Sara Simon
© Cover photos of Tansy Farrington-Wheeler by Pas Wheeler.

British Library Cataloguing in Publication Data.
A catalogue record for this book is available from the British Library.

### *Also by the same author:*
*Fields of Lavender* (poetry) 1991 ~ out of print.
*The Compassionate Years ~ history of the Royal New Zealand Society for the Protection of Animals*, RNZSPCA 1993
*Peaceful Pregnancy* CD, with Paul Robinson (The A Ffirm 1995)
*Howl at the Moon* (contributing poet), (Wild Women Press 1999)
*The Drinks Are On Me: everything your mother never told you about breast-feeding* (First edition published by Art of Change 2007)
[Second edition by Starflower Press 2008]
*Allattare Secondo Natura* (Italian translation of The Drinks Are On Me 2009) published by Terra Nuova www.terranuovaedizioni.it
*The Birthkeepers: reclaiming an ancient tradition* (Starflower Press 2008)
*Life Without School: the quiet revolution* (Starflower Press 2010), co-authored by Paul, Bethany and Eliza Robinson
*The Nurtured Family: ten threads of nurturing to weave through family life* (Starflower Press 2011)
*Natural Approaches to Healing Adrenal Fatigue* (Starflower Press 2011)
*Stretch Marks: selected articles from The Mother magazine 2002 – 2009*, co-edited with Paul Robinson (Starflower Press)
*The Mystic Cookfire: the sacred art of creating food for friends and family* (more than 260 vegetarian recipes) (Starflower Press 2011)
*The Blessingway: creating a beautiful Blessingway ceremony* (Starflower Press 2012)

Dedicated to:
*Topaz Mahalia*

Topaz, *a beautiful gemstone, which means joy and abundance*
Mahalia, *tender one*

## Acknowledgement
With immense gratitude to my parents,
Angelikah and Albertus
for gifting me a childhood in Nature.

# Gifts from Mother Nature

# Introduction

Mother Nature has long been my inspiration, nourishment and friend. She holds my hand and fills my soul. She's my daily companion. The Nature of my childhood in rural Australia is vastly different to the one I've lived in for the past decade and a half in the north of England.

My earliest Nature memory is standing outside during electrical storms in suburban Brisbane. I loved it! I'd raise my arms to the sky in excitement at those impulsive, dramatic displays of power and brilliance. The neighbours would call me 'crazy girl' and tell me to go inside. Storms like this were dangerous. They could kill me! I wasn't scared. I was alive. This was exciting!

Not long after, we left the suburbs and moved to 700 acres of land on the Darling Downs in South East Queensland. This would be my playground for ten years, until I left home at the age of 16 and moved to the Adelaide Hills in South Australia. Those ten years of my childhood are etched into every cell of my being. I explored the bushland, played on the granite rocks of a freshwater creek at the base of eucalyptus and wattle-covered mountains, climbed Pepperina trees, sucked on wild lemons, felt the red earth beneath my bare feet, avoided red-belly black snakes, imitated the bounding of kangaroos, rescued injured animals like crows and joeys, laughed with the kookaburras, brushed my cheeks against the soft maidenhair ferns which grew at the head of a waterfall, slept under the stars, and picked wild mushrooms (for the best soup you've ever tasted). My hair smelt of woodsmoke, drought-stricken days, and eucalyptus. I sipped lemongrass tea with my mother, swam in muddy dams, rode horseback up mountains, and felt the devastation and resurrection of the land around me following a bushfire. Nature invited me to be a writer. With her, I always felt at home.

I'm now in my mid-forties, and live in a 300-year-old sandstone cottage in the north of rural England with my husband and our two teenage home-educated daughters. Here, in the Eden Valley, I'm nourished by the fields and fells and the fertile river valley. Every day is brought into being by the sound of birdsong calling the Sun over the horizon. My garden puts me in touch with Mother Earth as I brush past the rapidly growing mint, and reach for the raspberries proffering their ruby jewels with abundance, plumpness and colour. I seek the plum trees for shade, and sink my hands into the black moist soil when enchanting my vegetable garden into the new growing year. Nasturtiums race to drape themselves over the compost heap, and blueberries beckon with dark temptations. Borage take over the vegetable beds with their delicate Renaissance-blue starflower petals and raspy cucumber-tasting leaves. On daisy-covered grass I can lie back and listen to birdsong from dawn to dusk. At sundown, the bats flitter back and forth, and the Moon rises before me, creating lunar tides in my body.

As a mother, Nature has played an important role in my parenting. During my pregnancy with Bethany, Paul and I travelled to the Bay of Islands to swim in the ocean with the dolphins. Born by candlelight in water, I should have known she'd be born under the sign of Pisces. It's ruled by the planet Neptune, which in astrology rules the oceans.

My daughters were worn in a baby carrier from birth, and so were with me or their father, in arms, wherever we went, whether that was walking through a Kauri forest or bathing in the ocean water by a black-sand beach on the North Island of New Zealand, walking past fields of sugar cane or pineapple plantations in Australia, or trekking down rural lanes during the snow in the far north of England. Together we've walked on an Irish bog, through an Italian peach orchard, and along a Devon beach.

In our home, our daughters grew up with a seasons table. Here, we would bring Nature to us, and each season would be displayed in all its beauty. Plump fuschia-coloured rosehips, pine cones, teasel, wild seeds and grasses, Autumn leaves, willow, stones and pebbles, moss and lichen, berries, pumpkin and squash, and so on, would adorn this sacred space.

From the world of Nature we find a living, breathing dictionary of inspiration from which to draw when choosing a name.

*Moss* might not seem like an obvious baby name to some. For you, however, memories of deep conversation and intimate connection in an ancient forest while sitting on moss with your best friend or lover could be all it takes to make moss one of the most beautiful words in the world. Why wouldn't you gift this to your baby? Maybe your child was born at home by the fire during an electrical storm and the lights went out. You birthed by candlelight. The Hindu name for lightning, *Ashani*, may call to you. Or maybe something from the Irish: *Mealla*, (f) [pr. MYAL] lightning, or *Áinfean*, (f) (pr. AWN f'yun] which means storm.

Who'd name a child after a tree, you might ask. If you were raised in the wilds of Alaska, then *Spruce* might call to you, or possibly *Alder*. Perhaps your grandmother was a forest warden and you spent many hours by her side exploring the belly of the pine-needle-fragrant forest floor. If trees enchant you, then maybe that's the obvious place to find your baby's name.

The first rays of sunlight come over the horizon as your baby takes her first breath and you breathe in her exquisite scent. This is a moment you'll remember forever. Dawn might be a more common girls' name, but perhaps you're more drawn to the name Sunrise? No? Then maybe *Anatoli*, (Russian) sunrise; *Cardinia*, (Australian aboriginal) dawn; *Kyeema*, (Australian aboriginal) of the dawn; *Zarya* or *Zaria*, (Russian) sunrise.

Your son or daughter might be born with hair the colour of fire, and so *Pyrrhus*, from the Greek, which means *flame-coloured*, could be your choice.

Some Nature names such as River and Savannah are becoming more used, yet there are just as many names we can draw upon, such as Prairie, Reef, Ridge.

Your baby might have been born during a rainbow, and although you love the meaning, the name doesn't attract you. Perhaps *Kahukura*, the Maori name for rainbow will be more attactive to you. Choosing a baby's name is a deeply creative and heartfelt process.

I hadn't yet met my Soul's Love when the name of my future daughter was 'given' to me. I say given because I don't feel I ever chose it. I was working at a school of metaphysics in Auckland, New Zealand, when the name Bethany jumped off the page. I'd never heard it before but something about it said 'this is your daughter's name'…and with those words, it would not leave me. It seemed rather odd, because I wasn't even in a relationship, but events followed that made it quite clear Bethany was already communicating with me from the spirit world and letting me know of her imminent arrival (she was born a year later).

I learnt that according to the Metaphysical Bible Dictionary, the esoteric meaning of Bethany is *House of Figs* ~ the overcoming of affliction. It's derived from the wailing sound of the foliage, and the 'tears' of the fruit (drops of gum). It comes from the Aramaic, and is recorded in the New Testament as the home of the siblings Mary, Martha, and Lazarus, as well as that of Simon the Leper.

The village of Bethany was the only place that was good to Jesus, who is said to have stayed there when he came to Jerusalem. The ancient Bethany was the site of an almshouse for the poor, and a place of care for the sick. Metaphysically, Bethany means the overcoming of affliction: "Whenever we make a mental demonstration we get a certain result in mind and body. In Bethany, Jesus raised Lazarus from the dead and thus overcame the sorrow, lamentation, and affliction of Martha and Mary".

My logical mind didn't want to use the name Bethany because of the temptation for people to shorten it to Beth... the name of one of my childhood bullies! So far, Bethany's name has remained intact, and she's very quick to stop people shortening it.

Bethany's middle name is Angelika, after my mother (who changed her name from Dagmar to Angelikah in midlife). It means *of the angels*, and is also a herb (angelica), so you'll find it in this book.

The name for my second child was to be Isaac Raphael. Isaac means *she laughed* (the Biblical Sarah didn't think she could be pregnant at the age of 90, and laughed when she found out), and Raphael is the archangel of healing. Raphael is also the middle name of one of my brothers, Rene, and I fell in love with the name as a child.

My second child turned out to be a daughter, and became *Eliza Serena* ~ names chosen by her father. Eliza is a diminuitive of Elizabeth, and means *pledged to God*. Eliza was the name of my husband's grandmother and great grandmother. And his mother was Elizabeth.

My mother's mother was *Liselotte*, which is the German name for Elizabeth. Without intention, both of our daughters have, diminuitively, carried on the name Elizabeth in the family line, drawing from both sides of the tree. Serena means *tranquil, serene*. It's from the Latin. In Spanish, it means *night dew*.

My birth name was Veronica Dagmar Sigrid Harbers. I'm the daughter of German parents, and sometime very early on in my childhood ~ about the age of five when I learnt to read and write ~ I decided to change the 'c' in Veronica to a 'k' as befits my Germanic origins. Clearly words and names were important to me from the start!

Veronica means *true image*. Saint Veronica is believed to have offered Jesus a cloth to wipe his face as he faltered on his way to crucifixion. She obtained a miraculous "true image" (in Latin "a vera icon") of Jesus's face on the cloth.

Veronica is also the name of a flower, so you will find it in this book. I never liked my name(s) as a child, but have grown to appreciate Veronika ~ particularly as it isn't very common. Perhaps it was the V sound that seemed a bit harsh, or maybe it felt too long to write, but I've really grown to value the meaning. I like to hear my name best when spoken by my husband and by the German women in my family ~ for some reason they make it sound so pretty.

Nicknames have always been lazy versions of Veronika: Vron (only two people in the world still get away with calling me that), and Ron ~ which I can't bear. I nip that in the bud very quickly when it happens. Oddly, it's always been boyfriends who shorten my name to Ron. Women, for some reason, go for Vron.

My initials spelt VDSH, and I was soon to learn how cruel schoolchildren can be with names! My 'friends' translated my initials to VD (as in *veneral disease*) Syphilis Herpes…a catalogue of sexual diseases is not a good affirmation for any child! Not surprisingly, I changed my middle names when I became a young adult. Latterly, this has been bittersweet.

Dagmar was my mother's birth name. In Danish it means *joy of the land*. In German, it means *glorious*, and in Norwegian and Swedish, it means *day*.

It has a beautiful meaning, and when said with a German accent is lovely to hear, but in my native Australia it was pronounced wrongly: DAG (rhymes with hag) and really exaggerated and over-emphasised) MAAAAAH (rhymes with char), and sounded so unbelievably ugly! I hated it! It made my skin crawl. I couldn't bear roll-call at school, and all the children having access to this part of me. I could never understand why I was given such a horrible name ~ until I became an adult and heard it said so beautifully by German women. To hear them say it brings tears to my eyes.

Sigrid is the name of one of my aunties. My father's sudden death in early 2012 really brought home to me the beauty of all of his sisters, and the link to that side of my family tree. The name Sigrid is from the Norse, and means *victorious, beautiful, fair*.

The middle name I chose for myself is Sophia. It's Greek for *wisdom*. I fell in love with the beautiful and feminine sound it makes when spoken. I felt I deserved that after a childhood of taunts!

As a child, I used to think the surname Robinson was so boring; so common. Well it would be compared to my maiden name of Harbers! I never met anyone else in childhood with my surname, which, incidentally, means *we have fought and we have conquered*. But, you know, the Universe always has the last laugh! Ah, the irony of marrying a man called Robinson! As it turns out, the name is very common ~ particularly where I live in the north of England, but I do appreciate its meaning: *famous brilliance*. What's not to love?

I'm one of eight children, and there's not a John or Mary amongst them: Wolfgang Reiner, Heidi Anita, Horst Albert, Ramona Rebecca, Kamahl, Rene Raphael, Albert Peter. Apart from Kamahl, who is now known as Kam (except by me!), the names have remained with them and I can't imagine them known as anything else. I remember my mother contemplating the name Jason when she was pregnant with Rene, but chose not to as there was a newsreader of that name and she felt it might be too common. I can't for a second see Rene as a Jason. I could have been a Daisy or Tamara. Who would I have been with either of those names? Would my personality have been different?

Our names do, indeed, identify us.

# *Who are you?*

Who are you? This universal question is almost certainly answered by your first name. Although we're more than our name, and are spiritual beings having a human experience, our name forms part of our human identity, and is what distinguishes us from (and connects us to) other people.

As a parent, naming our child is a huge responsibility. Few people are aware that the name we wear not only shapes our identity, but our future.

Studies in psychology show that parents tend to name their child based on something inherent within their genes, such as a sense of adventure or beauty or power. Does this then mean the child will be forced to live up to a parent's image, or will they grow into the energy of that name?

As an astrologer and numerologist, I feel that the name a child is given is one she wears for life (the energy continues even for women who change their surname in marriage). What if a child is given a name which doesn't feel comfortable to them or suit their self-image?

A person must feel good about their name. If a child doesn't like the name they've been given, it's highly likely they won't feel good about themselves. I often told my daughters while they were growing up that they were free to change their names if they didn't like them.

Why is our name so important? That is how people call to us. *We respond.* This essential part of identity brings up various considerations. Why did your parents choose your name? What is the origin of it? If you have a popular name, why did your parents choose that? Did they like it? Did they want to play it safe? Is your name unusual? Why did your parents choose that for you? Perhaps it has strong family connections going back generations.

Other important issues for parents to ponder are: will the name chosen for a baby be suitable throughout life? Will it 'work' when the baby becomes a teenager and a young adult? Will it fit in retirement? Will the chosen name invite peers to tease? With all of these questions, how do parents choose the right one for their baby?

Here are some simple guidelines to consider:

[] Always give your baby a meaningful name, and ideally one that has positive connotations. For example, I really love the name Reuben, but when I heard the meaning (a child born after a sibling has died), I knew it would never be a name I'd choose for a son of mine. Likewise, the pretty name Cassandra is one I'd never choose, because of its meaning in Greek Mythology: *she who entangles men*. Another meaning more positively suggests: *shining upon man*, while the English meaning for Cassie is *purity, unheeded prophetess*.

[] Avoid common names. You are giving your child a sense of identity.

[] Ensure the first name works well with the surname.

In my primary school, there were three boys named David in the class, so the teacher asked one of them to use his middle name, Graham, to avoid confusion. To this day, I'm saddened by this action. David changed from a sweet boy to a bully almost overnight. I'm not suggesting for a second that the name Graham means a bully, or there is anything wrong with that name, but the change of *identity* so abruptly, and by someone else, had a huge effect.

My best friend in school, Cherry, was named Višnja by her parents, but when she arrived in Australia from Croatia the school teacher suggested she change her name so that it would be easy for the other children to say. Two syllables: *vish nja*. Really, how hard is that? I know two-year-olds who can say Veronika clear as a bell, so I'm sure six year olds would have managed Višnja. As a regular guest in Cherry's home, she was both Cherry and Višnja to me, but I do feel that schoolteachers shouldn't tamper with children's given names. Višnja is Croatian for cherry, so while the words have the same meaning, energetically they sound very different.

In my late teens, I met a couple whose daughters were named Rainbow and Sunshine. I'd never heard of such names for children, but I admired their creativity. "How outrageous!" sniped the parishioners of my Lutheran boyfriend's congregation. I've come to understand that the meaning of a name is very important, and that is where the true beauty lies.

This book is different from other baby name books not only because it draws exclusively from Nature, but also because it isn't divided into girls' and boys' names. I believe names shouldn't be limited by other people's ideas of what is gender-appropriate. If a name calls to your imagination, then gift it to your child. In a few cases, I've included whether it's more suitable for one gender.

With some names, I've given the origin, language, meaning and pronounciation, especially where it isn't obvious. Many names, however, are self-evident e.g. Meadow, Reed, Ridge, Flower.

This is by no means a comprehensive list of Nature names, but I do hope it inspires you.

Choose a name for your baby because you love it, because it makes your heart sing. There'll always be people who don't like your choice. It's none of their business! This is your baby. The only people who have to like it are you and your partner, and hopefully the baby. Your chosen baby name will grow on everyone else in time, and it won't be long before they can't imagine your baby being called anything else. Many parents wouldn't dare pick a name until they met their baby, while others feel they've developed a relationship with their baby on the way to birth and have a sense of the right name early on.

This book is also a treasure-trove for adults unhappy with the name they've been given, and who'd like to change their name by deed poll to one they're more in harmony with. Novelists looking for interesting names for their characters will appreciate this addition to their resources.

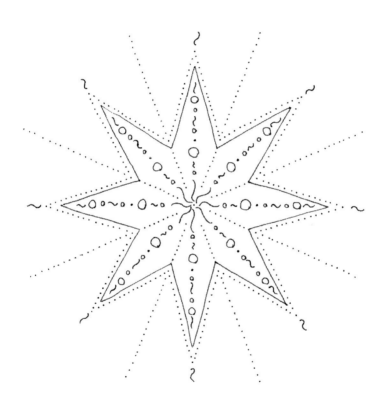

*Baby names inspired by Mother Nature*

# The Celestial and Time

*Starry, starry night.*
*Paint your palette blue and grey,*
*Look out on a Summer's day,*
*With eyes that know the darkness in my soul.*
*Shadows on the hills,*
*Sketch the trees and the daffodils,*
*Catch the breeze and the Winter chills,*
*In colours on the snowy linen land.*
Vincent, by Don McLean

As a child, I spent many evenings sleeping outside beneath the starry Australian skies with my mother. These are such precious memories for me. Together we shared the wonder of laying beneath night skies unaffected by light pollution, making wishes on falling stars. I knew the constellations of the Southern Hemisphere intimately. Many people feel insignificant when they stand under the vast starry sky. Not me.

On our kitchen wall we had the Desiderata, and the words left an indelible imprint on my growing mind:

*You are a child of the Universe,*
*no less than the trees and the stars;*
*you have a right to be here.*

Thank you, mum! I rejoice that I was given such a beautiful daily affirmation within the home, and in particular, being able to experience the truth of it at night time. The Celestial relates to the sky or visible heaven, as well as to the spiritual or invisible heaven. Although we see stars at night, they are there during the day time even though all we see is blue sky. The Sun travels through the constellations of the zodiac.

I don't wear a watch, and prefer to let time wear me rather than the other way around. My day is measured by the Earth's rhythm: sunrise, noon and sunset; my months measured by the lunar rhythms of my body's response to the Moon; and my year is marked by the seasons and Sabbats (holy days and wheels of the year).

Abrille, (Spanish) *April*
Adoni, (Australian aboriginal) *the sunset*
Akash, (Sanskrit) *the sky*
Alba, (Australian aboriginal) *a sand hill*
Alina, (Australian aboriginal) *the Moon*
Alinga, (Australian aboriginal) *the Sun*
Alkira, (Australian aboriginal) *the sky*
Allunga, (Australian aboriginal) *the Sun*
Alohilani, (Hawaiian) *bright sky*
Anatoli, (Russian) *sunrise*
Anil, (Sanskrit) *air*
Aoatea, (Maori) *dawn*
Araceli, *altar of the sky*
Atarangi, (Maori) *morning sky*
Aurora
Azura, (Persian) *blue sky*
Bertana, (Australian aboriginal) *the day*
Capricorn, *tenth sign of the zodiac, the mountain goat*
Cardinia, (Australian aboriginal) *dawn*
Celeste, (Latin) *celestial*
Comet
Cosmo
Cosmos
Cyrus, *the Sun*
Dagny, (Norwegian) *new day*
Danica, *morning star*
Dimitri (boy), (Russian) *Earth mother*
Dimitry, (both), (Russian) *Earth mother*
Drisana, (Hindu) *daughter of the Sun*
Eclipse
Equinox
Estelle, (Latin) *star*
Gaia, *Earth goddess*
Galaxy
Gedala, (Australian aboriginal) *the day*
Gulara, (Australian aboriginal) *moonlight*
Haru, (Japanese) *the Sun*
Haul, (Welsh) *the Sun*
Helina, (Russian) *light from the Sun*
Helios, (Greek) *the Sun*

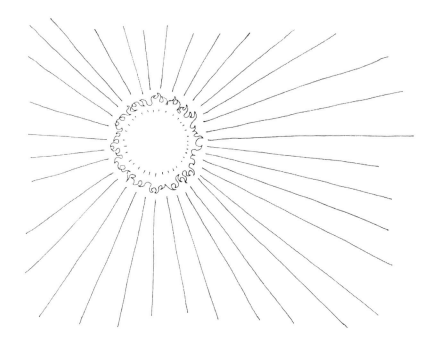

Hoata, (Maori) *the Moon on third night of lunar month*
Horizon
Hunu, (Maori) *Sunray*
Jannali, (Australian aboriginal) *the Moon*
Jiba, (Australian aboriginal) *the Moon*
Jupiter, *the largest planet in the sky*
Kakarauri, (Maori) *dusk; cloak of darkness*
Kalani, (Hawaiian) *the sky*
Kyeema, (Australian aboriginal) *of the dawn*
Lammas, *Sabbat (pagan wheel of the year) of the loaf-mass; celebration of the sacred grain*
Leo, *zodiac sign representing the lion*

Luna, *the Moon*
Marama, (Maori) *the Moon, light*
Mercury, *planet and God of communication and learning*
Meteor
Miah, (Australian aboriginal) *the Moon*
Midnight
Nebula
Neptune, *planet; it is the planet of spiritual love*
Noor, (Arabic) *light*
Orion
Ortzi, (Basque) *the sky*
Pluto, *god (and planet) of wealth*
Qamra, (Arabic) *the Moon*
Rangi, (Maori) *the sky*
Ravi, (Sanskrit) *the Sun*
Roxana, *dawn or little star*
Sabah, (Arabic) *the morning*
Sahar, (Arabic) *dawn*
Samson, *the Sun*
Sandya, (Hindu) *sunset*
Scintilla, (Italian) *sparkle*
Season, (Latin) *time of sowing*
Semine, (Danish) *Goddess of the Moon, Sun and stars*
Seren, (Welsh) *Star*
Shade
Shadow
Sidra, (Latin) *of the stars*
Sirius
Sita, (Sanskrit) *Hindu Goddess of the harvest*
Sitara, (Sanskrit) *morning star*
Skye, *sky*
Solana, (Spanish) *the Sun*
Solstice, *shortest and longest days of the year. Approximately 21st June, 21st September*
Somatra, (Hindu) *excelling the Moon*
Sonika, (Hindu) *golden*
Spica, (Latin) *name of a star*
Sora, (Japanese) *the sky*
Spiral, *examples are found throughout Nature, such as shells*
Starr, *star*

Sula, (Icelandic) *the Sun*
Surya, (Sanskrit) *the Sun*
Tangaroa, (Maori) *god of the sea*
Tautoru, (Maori) *belt of Orion*
Twilight, *the moments just after dusk*
Vasanti, (Sanskrit) *Spring*
Vega, (Arabic) *falling star*
Zaria, (Russian) *sunrise*
Zarya, (Russian) *sunrise*
Zelena, (Greek) *goddess of the Moon*
Zenith
Zephyr, (Greek) *west wind*
Zerlinda, (Hebrew) *a beautiful dawn*
Zodiac, *the twelve constellations in astrology*
Zoe, *life source*
Zora, (Slavonic) *dawn*

*Baby names inspired by Mother Nature*

# Geography & Landscape

I failed geography lessons in school, but the truth is I learnt everything I needed to know about the land by the life I lived when I wasn't inside the schoolroom walls. My father and mother moved us from the suburbs when I was a young girl, and we settled on 700 acres in rural Australia. The land taught me about the transitory nature of weather, natural disasters like floods and fire, and the elements, such as lightning. The soil varied from sunset red to coal black. I swam in dams, dive-bombed over a waterfall, trekked up mountains, rode horse-back, and ran barefoot across dry, drought-ridden fields. Living here taught me about the land, but also about human presence in such an environment. I understood the ecology of the land, and I have no doubt that a large part of my identity was shaped by my years there. Those mountains, hills, trees, scrubland, fields, dams and creek were the heartbeat of a dynamic child-hood.

Aaron, (Egyptian) *high mountain*
Adair, *oak tree ford*
Adam, *son of the red earth*
Adamah, (Hebrew) *earth*
Ahti, (Finnish) *god of the ocean*
Ailana, (Hawaiian) *island*
Ainakea, (Hawaiian) *white land*
Ainsley, *one's own meadow*
Alaina, (girl) (French) *rock*
Alaine, (boy) (French) *rock*
Alaska
Alba, (Australian aboriginal) *a sand hill*
Alepo'I, (Hawaiian) *surf, breaking waves*
Alpine
Alton, (Old English) *town at the river source*
Arctic, *northern polar region of the Earth*
Arden, *valley of the eagle*
Balun, (Australian aboriginal) *river*
Barina, (Australian aboriginal) *the summit*
Beck, *living beside a small stream*

Binda, (Australian aboriginal) *deep water*
Blair, *dweller on the plain*
Botany, *the study of plants*
Boulder
Brady, *broad meadow*
Brandon, *broom-covered hill*
Bryn, (Welsh) *hill*
Calhoun, *from the narrow forest*
Canyon
Cassius, *hollow*
Cheyenne, *mountain in Colorado, USA*
Clay
Cobar, (Australian aboriginal) *burnt earth*
Coral
Cordelia, *daughter of the sea*
Coreen, (Australian aboriginal) *the end of the hills*
Corowa, (Australian aboriginal) *a rocky river*
Crawford, *ford where crows gather*
Dagmar, (Danish) *joy of the land*
Daku, (Australian aboriginal) *sand*
Douglas, *black water*
Dylan, (Welsh) *son of the sea; great tide*
Echo
Ekala, (Australian aboriginal) *a lake*
Enakai, (Hawaiian) *glowing sea*
Enki, (Sumerian) *lord of the Earth*
Estuary, *partly enclosed coastal body of water with one or more rivers or streams flowing into it*
Flint, *form of mineral quartz*
Forrest
Ganan, (Australian aboriginal) *the west*
Garland, (Old English) *triangle land*
Glacier
Glaw, (Welsh) *rain*
Glenn, (Gaelic) *mountain valley*
Guinevere, *white shadow; white wave*
Ice

Indra, (Sanskrit) *possessing raindrops*
Katyin, (Australian aboriginal) *water*
Kun, (Chinese) *earth*
Lachlan, (Scottish) *land of the lakes*
Lance, (Germanic) *land*
Hadley, *heathery field*
Hadrian, (Latin) *of the Adriatic Sea*
Harlan, (Old English) *hare land*
Hayden, *heather-grown hill*
Heath, (Old English) *a moor*
Hinemoana, (Maori) *sea maiden*
Hirini, (Maori) *wide meadow*
Holden, *hollow valley*
India
Isla, (Scottish) *island*
Ivo, *yew wood*
Jordan, (Hebrew) *flow down*

Kai, (Japanese) *sea*
Kailani, (Hawaiian) *heavenly ocean*
Kelda, (old Norse) *a pool of deep still water*
Knox, *round hill*
Kodiak, (Russian) *island*
Kolora, (Australian aboriginal) *freshwater lagoon*
Lake
Lamilla, (Australian aboriginal) *a stone*
Landon, *long hill*
Lir (Irish) *god of the sea*
Logan, (Scottish) *little hollow*
Loinseach (m) (Irish) [pr. LUN shakh] *sea-farer*
Maayan, (Hebrew) *Spring water*
Mallee, (Australian aboriginal) *scrubland*
Marina, (Latin) *of the sea*
Marsh
Maxwell, *great stream*
Meadow
Mountain
Muirín, (m&f) )(Irish) [pr. MIR een] *born of the sea*
Murphy, *hound of the sea*
Mystic, *an unincorporated community in Nevada County, California; a village in New London County; a city in Appanoose County, Iowa; a river in eastern Massachusetts*
Nereus, (Greek) *god of the sea*
Ocean
Pelageya, (Russian) *open sea*
Pepik,(Russian) *stone*
Perry, *dweller near a pear tree*
Pierce, (Welsh) *rock*
Prairie
Radley, *red meadow*
Raleigh, *meadow of the roe deer*
Reef
Rere, (Maori) *waterfall*
Ridge
Ripley, *strip of clearing in the woods*
River
Roland, (Germanic) *famous land*
Roscoe, *deer forest*

Rylan, (Old English) *rye land*
Ryland, (English)*from the rye land;* (Irish) *island meadow*
Safiya, (African) *ocean*
Sagara, (Hindu) *ocean*
Sand
Sarita, (Hindu) *stream*
Savannah, (Native American) *open plain*
Shade
Sharni, *a flat plain*
Shaw, *small wood*
Shelley, *meadow's edge*
Shenandoah, *a valley in Virginia, USA*
Shirley, *bright meadow* (originally a boy's name)
Siberia
Sierra, (Spanish) *mountain*
Silas, *wood*
Silhouette
Tallis, *ancient forest*
Terra/Terran, *Earth*
Tundra
Tyrone, (Gaelic) *land of Eoghan; land of the noble*
Valonia, (Latin) *valley*
Wild
Wilde
Wilderness
Wood
Yardley, *fenced meadow*
Yuri, (Russian) *earth worker*
Zaire, *many rivers make one strong river*
Zhora, (Russian) *earth worker*

*Baby names inspired by Mother Nature*

# Colours

*Starry, starry night.*
*Flaming flowers that brightly blaze,*
*Swirling clouds in violet haze,*
*Reflect in Vincent's eyes of china blue.*
*Colours changing hue, morning field of amber grain,*
*Weathered faces lined in pain,*
*Are soothed beneath the artist's loving hand.*
Vincent, Don McLean


I'm not an artist, but I do have a deep appreciation of colour, and how light is absorbed and reflected. In childhood, I learnt about colour through thunder clouds so black I thought the world was ending; the wild apricot tree with fruits so juicy and colourful they appeared as miniature nectar-filled liquid sunsets; my chestnut mare whose mane I brushed so attentively; the luminous green of the maiden-hair ferns which grew at the waterfall's edge; the exquisite turquoise taffeta dress my mother lovingly sewed me; the white deaf kitten I had; the cocoa-coloured gills of the wild mushrooms we'd pick after the rain. Colour was all around me.


Amber, *halfway between yellow and red*
Auburn, *reddish brown*
Azure, *colour of the sky on a bright and clear day*
Bianca, (Italian) *light cream, off-white*
Bleu, (French) *Blue*
Chestnut
Ebony, *black/dark*
Gold
Hazel, *greenish-brown*
Indigo, *between violet and blue*
Maple
Ochre, *moderate yellow-orange earthy colour*
Olba, (Australian aboriginal) *red ochre*
Pyrrhus, (Greek) *flame-coloured*
Scarlet, *flaming red*

Sepia, *dark brown-grey colour, named after the rich brown pigment derived from the ink sac of the common cuttlefish (also a homeopathic remedy from the cuttlefish ink)*
Sienna, *(Italian) reddish brown*
Silver, *metallic colour tone resembling grey*
Turquoise, *bluish tone of light green*
Violet, *bluish-purple*

# Flowers

*When the night has been too lonely*
*And the road has been too long,*
*And you think that love is only*
*For the lucky and the strong,*
*Just remember in the Winter*
*Far beneath the bitter snows*
*Lies the seed that with the Sun's love*
*In the Spring becomes the rose.*
The Rose, Bette Midler

   I love to ask people what their favourite flowers are. Can they limit their answer to just one? I never can. The sunflower is bright, happy and, like me, follows the Sun. Freesias are exquisitely scented, and always remind me of my mother, for she grew them in our courtyard, where the heat from the Sun would draw out their fragrance. The lilac at my gate draws me in, making me wish I was a bee so I could sit on the blossoms all day long. And who doesn't love a rose? Starflowers (borage) make me smile with their perfect little star-shaped blossoms. Nasturtiums inspire me with their brilliant colours. Flowers allow us to beautify our homes, gardens and offices, and are used for food, ritual, medicine, romance, religion and vibrational medicine. I've never met a flower I didn't like.

Aciano, (Spanish) *bluebottle flower*
Akaisha, (Irish) *akaisha flower*
Alyssa
Amaranth, *family of colourful plants and flowers; a grain*
Anfisa, (Russian) *flower*
Araluen, (Australian aboriginal) *the water lily*
Aster
Azalea
Bláthnaid, (f) (Irish) [pr. BLAW nid] *flower*
Blossom
Bluebell
Calendula
Camellia

Celandine
Clover
Crisanta, *chrysanthemum*
Daffodil
Dahlia, (Swedish) flower or valley
Daisy
Fleur, (French) *flower*
Flora
Flower
Heather
Huhana, (Maori) *lily*
Hutukawa, (Maori) *flower of the Pohutukawa trea*
Ilima, (Hawaiian) *flower*
Iris
Jasmine
Jonquil
Leilani, *heavenly flower*
Lilac
Lillian
Lily
Lobelia
Lotus
Marguerite, *daisy or pearl*
Marigold
Myrtle
Orchid
Pansy
Petunia
Primrose
Rasine, (Polish) *rose*
Rose
Sadira, (Persian) *lotus*
Sakura, (Japanese) *cherry blossom*
Shoshana, (Hebrew) *rose or lily*
Tansy
Tulip
Valimai, (Welsh) *a mayflower*
Verbena, (Latin) *holy plant*
Veronica
Viola

Violet
Waratah, (Australian aboriginal) *a red flower*
Wisteria
Zagir, (Armenian) *a flower*
Zaira, (Arabic) *rose*
Zinnia

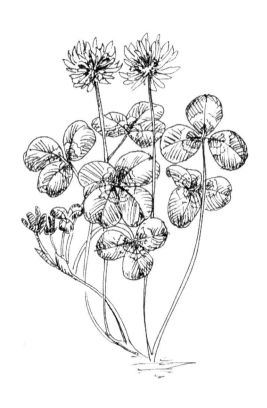

*The best time to plant a tree*
*was 20 years ago.*
*The next best time is now.*
~ Chinese Proverb

# Trees

*The trees are God's great alphabet:*
*With them He writes in shining green*
*Across the world His thoughts serene.*
~ Leonora Speyer

For the rest of my life, there will always be two trees that live in my heart: the pepperina, and the eucalyptus. These trees were the foundation of my childhood play. Under the pepperina I had two daughters: Kelly and Lucy, and I played with these imaginary girls for hours and hours. Up the pepperina tree, I had a secret hideaway and could see all the comings and goings to our home. The eucalyptus trees were everywhere on our property. My favourite eucalyptus memory, though, was when I lived briefly in Tasmania, as a young woman, and walked through a forest with my mother after a storm. The scent was the most beautiful and soul-enriching smell of my whole life. I shall never forget it.

Abilena, (Spanish) *Hazel*
Adair, (Gaelic) *from the oak tree ford*
Alameda, (Spanish) *poplar tree*
Alder, (German) *alder tree*
Ash
Aspen
Ayla, (Hebrew) *oak tree*
Bay
Beech
Berrigan, (Australian aboriginal) *wattle*
Birch
Birk, (Danish and Scottish) *Birch*
Burnu, (Australian aboriginal) *a tree*
Cedar
Conifer, *cone-bearing tree or shrub*
Cypress
Daphne, (Greek) *a laurel or bay tree*
Dubravka, (Croatian) *oak*
Ella, *oak tree*

*I think that I shall never see*
*A poem lovely as a tree.*
*A tree whose hungry mouth is prest*
*Against the Earth's sweet flowing breast;*
*A tree that looks at God all day*
*And lifts her leafy arms to pray;*
*A tree that may in Summer wear*
*A nest of robins in her hair;*
*Upon whose bosom snow has lain;*
*Who intimately lives with rain.*
*Poems are made by fools like me,*
*But only God can make a tree.*

~Joyce Kilmer, Trees, 1914


Elm
Ghera, (Australian aboriginal) *gum leaf*
Gideon, *feller of trees*
Hollis, (Old English) *holly tree*
Holly
Huckleberry or Huck
Hyacinth
Ilana, (Hebrew) *tree*
Iva, (Croatian) *willow*
Jacaranda
Jarrah, (Australian aboriginal) *type of eucalyptus*
Jasena, (Croatian) *ash tree*
Juniper
Kaleena, (Russian) *rowan tree*
Karri, (Australian aboriginal) *type of eucalyptus*
Karuah, (Australian aboriginal) *type of wild plum tree*
Kauri, (Polynesian) *New Zealand tree*
Keziah, *cassia tree*
Kiri, (Maori) *tree bark*
Kylie, (Australian aboriginal) *a boomerang ~ made from wood*
Larch
Laurel

Lemana, (Australian aboriginal) *the She-Oak tree* (She Oak is used in vibrational medicine for infertility)
Linden
Lovorka, (Croatian) *laurel*
Magnolia
Maple
Nash, *by the ash tree*
Oak
Oleander
Pine
Poplar
Rohana, (Sanskrit) *sandalwood*
Rowan
Sequoia
Spindle
Spruce
Taree, (Australian aboriginal) *a wild fig*
Vernon, (Norse) *place of alders*
Yarrah, (Australian aboriginal) *a river red gum*
Yvette, (French) *yew tree*

*Trees are poems that Earth writes upon the sky,*
*We fell them down and turn them into paper,*
*That we may record our emptiness.*

~ Kahlil Gibran

*Baby names inspired by Mother Nature*

# Plants

My first memory of plants is of the ferns we grew in the front of our home. They had long fronds, and for some reason I used to pick the leaves and pretend they were money. I still have the urge when I see that particular fern ~ forty years later!

As a child, I remember walking through the fields one dark moonless night with my dad and ending up marching right into a large patch of nettles! OUCH! I've since learned that the best cure for nettle stings is to rub the juice of dock leaves on the rash. Amazingly, Mother Nature grows dock leaves wherever there are nettles. These days I grow nettles in my garden to feed the wildlife, and to make tea or soup from in the Spring. It's a wonderful source of dietary iron.

Antea, *wild rose*
Arnica
Betony
Bramble
Briar
Briony, (Greek) *climbing plant*
Bryonia
Buddleia, *butterfly bush*
Chicory
Cotton
Cynara, *thistly plant*
Elodie, *marsh flower*
Fern
Fireweed
Flax
Foliage, *a cluster of leaves*
Harakeke, (Maori) *New Zealand flax*
Heather
Hemlock
Hemp, *cannabis sativa*
Henna, *a flowering plant used for centuries to dye skin, hair, finger-nails and wool*
Honesty
Ivy

Jessamy, *jasmine flower*
Kirra, (Australian aboriginal) *leaf*
Leaf/Leif
Lichen (pronounced *like en*)
Mistletoe
Moss
Myrtle
Nettle
Omer, *sheaf of corn*
Papyrus
Petal
Petani, (Maori) *house of figs* [form of Bethany]
Reed
Rosehip
Sabra, *prickly pear*
Sage
Teasel
Vanilla
Vidonia, (Portugese) *a vine branch*
Vine
Wildflower
Wintergreen
Yarrow

# Herbs, Spices and Seasonings

My mother grew lemongrass in our garden. This herb grows to about three feet, and its lemon-scented leaves make beautiful tea. It's used widely in Thai cooking, as well as in alternative therapies as an antimicrobial and antifungal.

I loved to pick fresh curly-leaved parsley from the garden so my mother could finely chop it on top of our tomato soup. It's funny what smells and memories from childhood stay with you. I can't pick or chop parsley without my mother and tomato soup being right there in the kitchen with me.

Angelica
Anise
Basil
Bay Laurel
Borage
Cajun
Calendula
Cardamom
Carraway
Cayenne
Chamomile
Chicory
Chilli
Cinnamon

Clove
Comfrey
Coriander
Cumin
Edelweiss
Fennel
Geranium
Ginger
Hawthorn
Honey
Juniper
Lavender
Loveage
Mace
Marjoram
Mel (Welsh) *honey*
Noni
Olida
Paprika
Pepper
Poppy seed
Primrose
Rihana, (Arabic) *sweet basil*
Rosemary
Shako, (Native American) *mint*

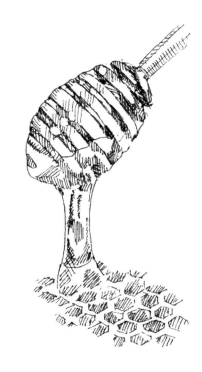

*What are little girls made of?*
*Sugar and spice, and everything nice,*
*That's what little girls are made of.*

*"And God said, Behold, I have given you every
herb-bearing seed which is upon the face of all the Earth,
and every tree, in the which is the fruit of a tree-yielding seed;
to you it shall be for meat"*

~ The Holy Bible

Saffron
Sage
Salvia
Senna
Star Anise
Starflower, *borage*
Sorrel
Tamarind
Tarragon
Thyme
Tulsi
Tumeric or Turmeric
Valerian
Verbena

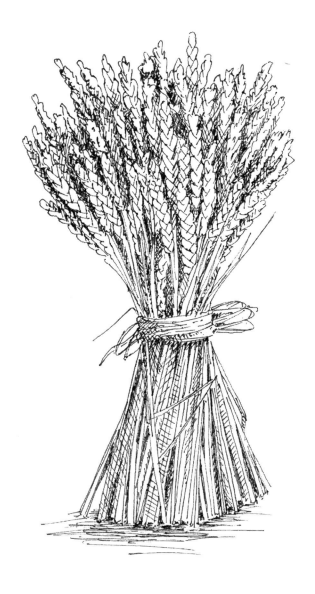

*Baby names inspired by Mother Nature*

# Fruit, Vegetables and Grains

*Happiness is sharing a bowl of cherries*
*and a book of poetry with a shade tree.*

~ Terri Guillemets

My mother worked long and hard to create a veritable Garden of Eden for her family. Fruits included: carob, pear, apple, orange, avocado, cherry, olive, banana, paw paw (paypaya), mandarin, quince, custard apples, pomegranate and more. Some trees took on special meaning, such as the pear tree which had my baby brother's placenta buried beneath it. Something about his home birth, and the organ which nourished his womb life, living on in our garden seemed magical to my ten- year-old mind.

The first time I ever tasted an olive was straight from our trees. My mother had told me not to pick them, but I couldn't resist. YUK! It was a very long time before I ate olives again. They need to be cured in brine to make them edible. My youngest daughter, Eliza, loved olives right from toddlerhood, and would always request them as a snack when we were shopping in town. At the olive stall, she could never take just one from the samples but a whole handful: a big, chubby, dimple-fingered handful!

Afina, (Romanian) *blueberry*
Aluma, *maiden; sheaf of grain at harvest*
Amaranth
Aviv, *young grain*
Aviva, *young grain*
Barric, *grain farm*
Basmati
Berry
Carob
Cherry
Cerise, (French) *cherry*
Citron, (French) *lemon*

Clementine
Cocoa
Cranberry
Dagan, *grain; the earth*
Dunja, (Croatian) *quince*
Garner, *to gather grain/who helped harvest grain*
Goren, *grain harvest*
Graine, *grain*
Harvest
Jagoda, (Croatian) *strawberry*
Kasha, *Middle Eastern grain*
Maple, *syrup*
Miller, *one who grinds grain*
Millet
Mirta, (Croatian) *myrtle*
Nectar, *sugar-rich liquid from plants*
Olive
Omri, (Hebrew) *sheaf of grain*
Pollen
Pomegranate
Quinoa (pronounced keen-wa) *Mother of Grains*
Rye, *grain used for bread and whiskey*
Višnja, (Croatian) *wild cherry*
Zea, (Latin) *ripened grain*
Zia, *light, splendour, grain*

*A seed hidden in the heart of an apple*
*is an orchard invisible.*
~ Welsh Proverb

# Animals

I'm a cat woman through and through, and when I'm in my nineties I'll still be living with cats. Their purr, their companionship, the way they play in the garden, all bring joy to my heart. As a child, we had dozens of cats at one point when all the fertile females had kittens. My family and I currently live with three very charming cats. As a child, I would love to wake to the sight of a kangaroo in the garden or a red fox or black dingo slinking into the scrubland. The storm bird, rarely heard, would indicate the coming of rain.

Aandaleeb, (Sanskrit) *bird*
Abejundio, (Spanish) *bee*
Akala, (Australian aboriginal) *parrot*
Akama, (Australian aboriginal) *whale*
Akilina, (Russian) *like an eagle*
Arinya, (Australian aboriginal) *kangaroo*
Ava, (Latin) *bird*
Banjora, (Australian aboriginal) *koala*
Bruin, (Welsh) *bear*
Burilda, (Australian aboriginal)
*black swan*
Cobra
Colm, (Gaelic) *dove*
Conall, (Irish/Scottish) *wolf*
Coyote
Drake, *dragon or a male duck*
Dove
Eerin, (Australian aboriginal) *a small grey owl*
Fawn
Feather
Fox
Hawk
Io lani, (Hawaiian) *royal hawk*
Kaiwharawha, (Maori) *feather from an albatross*
Kami, (Australian aboriginal) *prickly lizard*
Kobra, *variation of Cobra*
Kolet, (Australian aboriginal) *dove*

Lark
Leonid, (Russian) *lion*
Lynx
Madryn, (Welsh) *fox*
Mato, (Sioux) *bear*
Oriel, (Latin) *oriole bird*
Otter
Raven
Robin
Ruru, (Maori) *owl*
Sable
Sabre
Schmetterling, (German), *butterfly*
Serica, (Latin) *the silken one*
Shell
Shika, (Japanese) *deer*
Simba, (Swahili) *lion*
Tui, (Maori) *honeyeater bird*
Vana, (Polynesian) *sea urchin*
Wolf
Wren
Yael/Yaelle, (Hebrew) *ibex* (mountain goat)

# Weather & Seasons

Sitting on the wooden verandah, aged about nine, I waited expectantly for the approaching storm. Sinister black clouds forced their way across the sky. Clapping thunder beat a marching drum. Lightning set the air alive. And with the first drops of heavy rain I saw hail stones on the lawn. WOW! They were *huge*! It didn't take me long, though, to figure out they were ice cubes thrown from the window by my older sister Heidi. Sisters!

Drought reminds me of those seven long years with no rain, and the many times my mother encouraged us children to do a rain dance.

Frost invites me to imagine a world of ice fairies and magical kingdoms. The first time I saw frost as a child, it was outside my bedroom window in our new home in the country. It was a moonlit evening, and the frost shone on each eucalyptus leaf like diamonds. I crept out of bed believing it to be snow.

England is a country with definable seasons. My favourite? How could it not be Summer? Actually, the English Summer generally disappoints me due to the lack of decent hot temperatures, but I do love to potter in my garden at the height of the season. Autumn brings mixed blessings: a profusion of colour, a beauty to the light, sunny days and crisp evenings; an abundance of golden leaves...and the promise (or is that a threat?) of the long cold months ahead. I complain bitterly in the Winter as I have zero tolerance for the cold, but as a lover of words it's the perfect season for snuggling by the fire and reading for hours on end, or crafting new books. Baking gingerbread or a pot of root vegetable soup simmering on the stove brings out the best of these icy days. Spring, now there's a season to love. Fresh, new, exciting, and full of promise. Bulbs emerge, leaves unfurl, lambs are born. Life is for living.

Áinfean, (f) (Irish) (pr. AWN f'yun] *storm*
Amiri, (Maori) *gentle wind from the East*
Amirina, (Australian aboriginal) *rain*
Aromahana, (Maori) *springtime*
Ashani, (Hindu) *lightning*

Autumn, *season heralding the end of Summer and preparing for Winter*
Barega, (Australian aboriginal) *wind*
Brisa, (Spanish) *breeze*
Bronte, *thunder*
Camira, (Australian aboriginal) *wind*
Claudia, (German) *cloudy day*
Cloud
Damini, (Hindu) *lightning*

Darel, (Australian aboriginal) *blue sky*
Dgwaagi Bkwene, (Ojibwe) *Autumn haze*
Dima, (Russian) *torrential rain*
Dimah, (Russian) *torrential rain*
Eira, (Welsh) *snow*
Ella, *beautiful fairy maiden* (used when born near Beltane)
Frost
Hauku, (Maori) *dew*
Indra, *possessing drops of rain*
Iorangi, (Maori) *cirrus cloud*

Kahukura, (Maori) *rainbow*
Kolya, (Australian aboriginal) *Winter*
Leewana, (Australian aboriginal) *wind*
Lilleth, *goddess of storms*
Mazin, (Arabic) *rain clouds*
Mealla, (f) (Irish) [pr. MYAL] *lightning*
Mirrin, (Australian aboriginal) *a cloud*
Misty
Neva, (Spanish) *snow*
Phirun, (Khmer) *rain*
Rain/Raine
Rainbow
Sefarina, *gentle wind*
Spring
Storm
Summer
Sunshine
Talia, (Hebrew) *morning dew*
Tallara, (Australian aboriginal) *rain*
Tiân haf, (Welsh) *heavenly Summer*
Tornado
Varsha, (Hindu) *a shower of rain*
Winter
Zephyr, *a gentle breeze*
Zephyrus (Greek mythology) *god of the West wind who brings gentle Spring*
Ziazan, (Armenian) *rainbow*

# Gems, Crystals and Precious Stones

Agate
Amber
Amethyst
Beryl
Cinnabar
Citrine
Crystal
Diamond
Emerald
Garnet
Gemma, (Latin) *precious stone*
Gold
Jade, *green stone which offers protection and friendship*
Jasper
Jewel
Malachite
Onyx
Opal
Pearl
Quartz
Ruby, *red gemstone*
Sapphire, also Safira, Saphira, Sapphira and Sephira. *Biblically, the gems represented the foundation pavings of the universal heavens, described as the throne of God.*
Silver
Tiger's Eye
Topaz, *abundance and joy*
Tourmaline
Turquoise

# Natural Fibres

Natural fibres have been essential to human life since the beginning of civilisation. Excavations in Mexico and Pakistan show that cotton was being used in 5000BC, while Chinese history shows the use of silk began around the 27th century BC. Jute (also known as hessian or burlap) has been used since the beginning of human life. Fibres are produced by plants or animals, and are then spun into rope, thread or filament. This can then be used to matt, weave, knit or bond.

Abaca, *plant fibre*
Alpaca, *wool from the alpaca*
Angora, *white wool from the angora rabbit*
Camel
Cashmere
Coir, *fibre from coconut shells*
Cotton, *plant fibre*
Flax
Hemp
Hessian (pronounced *hesh an* or *hess ee an*)
Jute
Mohair
Rami
Silk
Sisal

# Fire

Fire can conjure up so many memories. In childhood, I saw its devastating face through the third-degree burns it left on my father's skin after he'd tried to save people from a burning hut in Papua and New Guinea.

Bushfires ripped through our mountains when I was young, and destroyed every living thing it could catch: kangaroos, koalas, lizards, snakes, mice, trees, bushes. From the charred remains, new life grew more abundantly and lush than before. My first lesson in transformation.

As a young woman, I participated in fire-walking workshops ~ walking on hot coals is a life-changing experience. To know you can walk on them shows you that just about anything is achievable.

I love the flickering light of a campfire, and the colour and warmth of our hearth during Winter, while a small flame on a beeswax candle instantly calms me. As an astrologer, I look at a person's birth chart and can see their level of drive and passion based on the presence or absence of fire signs (Aries, Leo, Sagittarius) and fire planets (Mars, Sun, Jupiter).

Adar, (Hebrew) *fire*
Agni, (Sanskrit) *fire*
Aiden, (Old Irish) *fire*
Blaize
Brenton, (Old English) *fire town*
Conleth, (Irish) *chaste fire*
Ember
Fintan, (Irish) *white fire*
Flame
Kala, (Australian aboriginal) *fire*
Kari, (Australian aboriginal) *smoke*
Kimba, (Australian aboriginal) *bush fire*
Maka, (Australian aboriginal) *a small fire*
Phoenix, *mythical bird which rises from the ashes. Associated with Scorpio in the zodiac*
Smoke
Smokey

# About the artist

Sara Simon is a lifelong artist whose creativity was encouraged from an early age, and who rarely goes anywhere without a sketchbook and pencil. After Art College, she detoured, in the Nineties, via a degree and employment in graphic design, but returned to paint and paper after becoming a mother and rejoining what she considers her true creative path. Today her arts include painting, drawing, writing, sewing, baking and too many other expressions to list.

Inspired by the outdoors, other people and the experiences of life, she's also devoted to gentle living and conscious parenting. Sara works from home in the Peak District, UK, where she lives with her husband and two sons. This is her second collaboration with Veronika. She illustrated *The Mystic Cookfire: the sacred art of creating food to nurture friends and family*.

# About the author

Veronika Robinson is married to the love of her life, Paul, and together they have two inspiring home-educated teenage daughters. They live in an old farmhouse in the beautiful Eden Valley, Cumbria, and edit an international magazine on parenting. She loves the outdoors, and has planted many trees

during her life. Veronika is never happier than when her hands are in the dark, moist soil and there's warm sunshine on her skin, or when she's picking fresh blueberries or raspberries from the garden. Other passions include psychological astrology, cello music, reading and writing, gardening by the Moon, long chats on the phone with friends, cooking up a storm in the kitchen with her daughters, and walking hand-in-hand with her husband. Her mother and father provided her with the BEST childhood, amongst the gum trees, kangaroos, blazing sunshine, and mountains ~ and for this, she will be eternally grateful. Veronika loves words and names, and is always thrilled when her daughter Bethany, a composer, offers her music to title. Veronika has favourite names for another five children and twenty cats, but isn't planning any more of either. Maybe just one more cat called *Italics*.

# Starflower Press

Starflower Press is dedicated to publishing material which lifts the heart, and helps to raise human consciousness to a new level of awareness. It draws its name and inspiration from the olden-day herb, Borage (Borago Officinalis), commonly known as Starflower, which is still found in many places, though it's often thought of as a wild flower, rather than a herb. Starflower is recognisable by its beautiful star-like flowers, which are formed by five petals of intense blue (sometimes it's pink). The unusual blue colour was used in Renaissance paintings. The Biblical meaning of this blue is *heavenly grace*. Borage, from the Celt: borrach, means *courage*. Throughout history, Starflower has been associated with courage. It's used as a food, tea, tincture and flower essence to bring joy to the heart and gladden the mind. For other books by the author, visit www.starflowerpress.com

Veronika and Sara can be contacted through Starflower Press. email: office@starflowerpress.com

# The Mother magazine

The Mother magazine focuses on integrated optimal health, well-being, conscious family connection, and holistic living. The purpose of this publication isn't to prescribe a way of parenting, but to help women and men access their deep, intuitive knowing, and find a way to parent optimally. The Mother covers many topics and aspects of natural family living, from conscious conception and fertility awareness, to organic birth and death, peaceful pregnancy, human-scale education, natural beauty and cleaning products and toys, vaccine awareness and natural immunity, teenagers, rites of passage, electromagnetic radiation, Moontime, full-term breastfeeding, the family bed and attachment parenting. We recognise that modern technology is here to stay, and we aim to inform readers about how this can impact on a child's well-being and development. At times, most of us compromise the optimal, both in terms of parenting, and life in general. At The Mother, we encourage taking responsibility for the outcomes of our choices, actions and inaction. If you've enjoyed reading *Baby Names Inspired by Mother Nature*, then we invite you to join The Mother magazine's family. Subscriptions available worldwide:
www.themothermagazine.co.uk or
www.themothermagazine.org (for USA and Canada.)
To have a mentoring session with Veronika on any aspect of natural parenting, visit: www.veronikarobinson.com